FOLK ART

Mary Moody

CRESCENT BOOKS
NEW YORK • AVENEL, NEW JERSEY

Frontispiece: In the Dutch Hinderloopen style, an intricately painted coffee grinder by Ann Mairec.

Special thanks to Annie Holcombe, Mountain Living and Pamela Andrews, Fairlight Folk Art Studio.

This 1994 edition published by Crescent Books,
distributed by Random House Value Publishing, Inc.,
40 Engelhard Avenue, Avenel, New Jersey 07001.

Random House
New York • Toronto • London • Sydney • Auckland

First published in 1992
Reprinted in 1993
Reprinted in 1994

© Copyright Harlaxton Publishing Ltd
© Copyright design Harlaxton Publishing Ltd

Publishing Manager: Robin Burgess
Project Coordinator: Mary Moody
Editor: Dulcie Andrews
Illustrator: Kathie Baxter Smith
Designed & produced for the publisher by Phillip Mathews Publishers
Typeset in the U.K. by Seller's
Produced in Singapore by Imago

Title: Country Crafts Series: Folk Art
ISBN: 0 517 10254 4

CONTENTS

INTRODUCTION

Through this Country Craft series, it is our hope that you will find satisfaction and enjoyment in learning a new skill. In this case, that of folk art.

Folk art is simply a method of applying a decorative painted surface to timber or metal to create objects of great beauty and homey charm. Folk painting has a long and fascinating history, and particular regional styles have developed that provide a wealth of detail for inspiration. However, newcomers to the craft should not feel inhibited by these traditions, in terms of developing an individual style that is unique and distinctive.

Literally, folk art is "painting of the people," and it is this quality that makes it accessible and achievable for so many enthusiasts. As folk art traditions are based on the work of untrained artists, it is therefore a style and technique that can be emulated by painters who may never have picked up a paintbrush before embarking on this creative and satisfying craft.

Once you have mastered the basic techniques described in this book, with a little practice and patience, you will develop the skills to create your own beautifully crafted pieces.

Opposite: A variety of stylized cats from pre-cut timber shapes with semi-realistic, floral and modern designs.

GETTING STARTED

FOR CENTURIES in eastern Europe, peasant people painted their simple pine furniture, both as a decorative device and to provide protection for the comparatively soft timber surface. Plain pine was generally the only building material available to these peasants and it proved an ideal background for their artistic endeavors.

As untrained artists, they were not concerned with the formal rules of painting. Perspective and proportion were overlooked, and this gave the work the naive, child-like quality that is so refreshing. Indeed, realism is the last requirement of folk art, as can be seen in some traditional works that feature flowers much larger than the people represented in the same painting. Roses are sometimes seen emerging from the same plant as tulips, demonstrating a very broad artistic license.

Village life and nature are the main themes of traditional folk art painting. Religious festivals and beliefs were often incorporated into paintings in a symbolic way, and many repetitive themes were highly stylized.

There is some disagreement about the origins of folk art, but it is generally thought to have been produced in Germany. The German word *Bauernmalerei* means "peasant painting" and this is the term used to describe the Bavarian folk art we know today. It was mainly practiced in the alpine areas of Germany, Switzerland and Austria, as the long, restrictive winter months gave the artists plenty of time to complete their works.

Initially, the style of painting was an imitation of the more expensive hardwood furniture seen in the homes of the wealthy, and the paintings actually copied woodgrains and included clever representations of flatwood carving and timber inlay. However, as the craft progressed, it became more colorful and adventurous. Some believe it emulated the style of bright paintings on the wooden ceilings of village churches and some country castles.

Styles varied from region to region, and each country developed its own distinctive style, by which old works can still be categorized. Some are very stark and somber, some rich and floral, others are more formal with symmetrical patterns and designs.

Eventually the craft travelled to North America, where cold winters again provided an opportunity for European immigrant farmers to work at their craft. In areas such as Pennsylvania it was as popular as patchwork quilting, and many fine examples of early folk artists' work can still be seen today.

Opposite: This small cabinet, thimble, and darning mushroom, painted by Elizabeth White, present a charming contrast to the usual bright colors of folk art.

GLOSSARY

Acrylic paints: Fast-drying, water-based paints used extensively in folk art painting.

Antiquing: A method used to give the finished painted piece an "aged" appearance, softening the brightness of the colors.

Basecoating: A solid background color applied before painting the design.

Bauernmalerei: The German word for peasant painting.

Brush basin: A professional water bowl that protects brushes and helps to keep them clean.

Comma: A teardrop-shaped brush-stroke used frequently in folk art painting.

Crackling: A clear coat applied after painting to produce a cracked "aged" effect.

Crescent: A curved brushstroke used frequently in folk art painting.

Dry shading: A shading technique using paint without water.

Flat brush: A paintbrush with a square end.

Freehand: A method of painting directly onto the work, without first tracing a design or pattern.

Glaze: A semi-transparent layer applied over the painted project.

Layered painting: A technique of painting and shading in layers.

Load: To add paint to a brush, or sponge.

Liner brush: A round brush used for fine linework.

Naive: A simple, child-like painting style developed by untrained artists.

Palette: A board for mixing paint colors.

These bright and colorful Christmas boxes and decorations make excellent gifts.

Pickling: A semi-transparent treatment used on wood to give it a light appearance prior to painting.

Polyurethane: A hard, clear surface used as a finish for projects that need to be waterproof or heatproof.

Round brush: A paintbrush with a pointed end.

Side-loading: A painting technique where more than one color is loaded onto the brush, to create shading in one brushstroke.

Spattering: A technique using a toothbrush to spatter paint on a surface prior to painting the design.

Spatula: A wooden or plastic implement used for mixing paint colors together.

Sponging: A technique using a sponge loaded with paint to create interesting patterns prior to painting the design.

Tracing paper: A semi-transparent paper used to trace and then transfer designs onto a project.

Varnish: A clear water-based finishing coat used to protect the completed painting.

Wet shading: A shading technique using layers of wet paint.

Pre-cut timber shapes are ideal for beginner's projects. The naive box seen here was painted by ten-year-old Llew Jones.

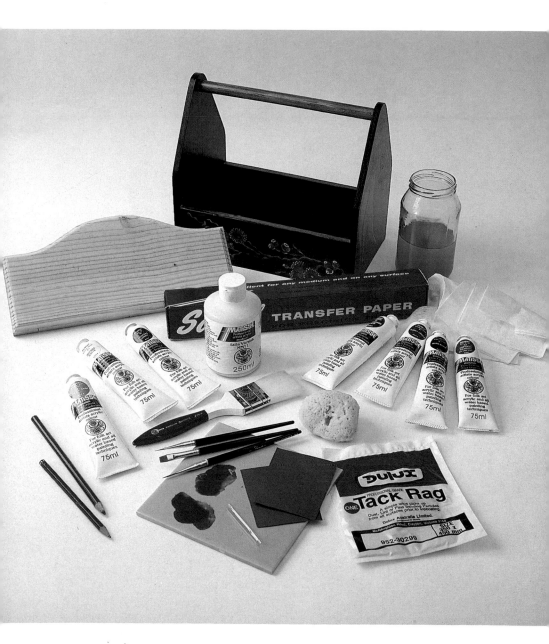

Basic requirements for folk art painting include acrylic water-based paints, brushes, tracing paper, a sponge, tack rag, pencils, a palette and water-based varnish for the finishing coat.

TOOLS AND MATERIALS

CRAFT EQUIPMENT and supplies can be very expensive, however, folk art beginners can make do with certain improvised equipment to reduce costs. Then, if they become serious about continuing to paint, more expensive semi-professional equipment can be purchased.

THE BASICS

Most of the equipment listed below is available in general hobby stores, art suppliers or specialty folk art stores – sometimes these specialty stores are owned and operated by teachers of folk art, and information about courses may be available.

Paints　Essentially, a beginner should invest in about eight basic colors, then build up a range of additional colors gradually. Folk art paint is water-based acrylic, and most brands are both non-toxic and environmentally friendly. Ask about these qualities at the time of purchase.

The standard color range for a beginner should include black, white, red, yellow, blue, green, brown and ochre. The range of additional colors is enormous, and includes glorious shades of violet, coral, pearl white, burnt umber and phthalo blue.

Acrylic paint is useful because it dries quickly (generally in 20 minutes) and the cleaning of brushes can be done with water. If a mistake is made while painting, it can be quickly erased by wiping the area clean with a damp paper towel before it has time to dry. Always take care to wipe the tops of the paint tubes each time they are used and screw the lids back on firmly.

Palettes　Professional folk artists use a palette that is designed to keep the paint moist for long periods, even days at a time. However, beginners can use something as simple as the plastic lid of an ice cream container or margarine tub. Never squeeze too much paint onto the palette in case there is an interruption – remember the paint will dry out quickly.

Brushes　Most artists agree that investing in good quality brushes is worthwhile, even for the beginner. Cheap brushes will rapidly lose their refined edge and brush hairs will drop out, adhering to the paint surface. Good quality brushes will help insure good brushstrokes, and this in turn will improve the quality of the work.

The beginner will need a range of brushes, from a very fine No.00 liner brush, to a thick brush for basecoating and applying the finishing varnish. It is important that the fine brushes are of a good quality, as they are used for painting detail. The wider brushes can be the less expensive synthetic variety.

A BASIC BRUSH KIT SHOULD INCLUDE:

1	NO. 00 LINER BRUSH
1	NO. 2 ROUND BRUSH
1	NO. 4 ROUND BRUSH
1	NO. 6 FLAT BRUSH
2	LARGE SYNTHETIC BRUSHES

BASIC RANGE OF FOLK ART BRUSHES

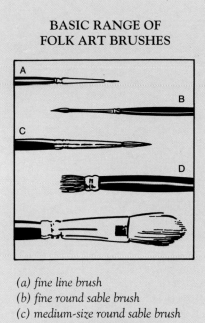

(a) *fine line brush*
(b) *fine round sable brush*
(c) *medium-size round sable brush*
(d) *medium-size flat brush*
(e) *one or two inexpensive large synthetic brushes*

Leaving brushes to stand in a jar can result in bent bristles.

Care of brushes is important if they are to stay in good condition. Avoid leaving brushes sitting in water for any length of time, and when painting has finished for the day, wash them out well in warm (never hot) soapy water, making sure all the soap is rinsed out thoroughly.

Do not use brushes to mix paint, as this will make them dog-eared. Use a spatula instead. And if a brush eventually loses its point, save it for a special soft-edged effect like tree foliage.

Water bowl Commonly, a glass jar is used for washing brushes; however, professionals invest in a "brush basin" which has a ridged base which helps to clean brushes every time they are rinsed. The grooves in the side of the bowl stop the brushes from developing curled points while they are resting in the water.

Sealer/varnish Finished works must be sealed with a clear finish to protect the paintwork. A water-based, satin-finish varnish is most often used, although a gloss finish is also available for a specific look (e.g. Russian folk art.) The finishing techniques vary from one style to another (see "Finishing Techniques".)

Sandpaper A range of sandpaper grades is useful for sanding rough timber or smoothing surfaces prior to basecoating.

Tracing paper Opaque tracing paper is used for copying a design from a book or magazine onto the item to be painted.

Pencils Sharp pencils produce a fine, accurate line when outlining the design on the tracing paper.

Sponges The texture of the sponge creates interesting paint effects.

Spatula This makes it easy to mix paints on the palette.

A plate decorated in the Ukranian Petrakiuka-style. The background has been pickled and the rim edged with a classical floral border.

Extras   Other useful items are paper towels, a hand towel, cotton swabs and cellophane tape, and a tack rag for dusting in between coats of paint or varnish.

WHAT TO PAINT

Items suitable for folk art painting are many and varied. Hobby stores carry a wide range of specially made objects for painting, from simple boxes in every possible shape and size, to wall hangings, animal cutouts, plaques, doorstops, pins, bangles, coathangers and even clocks.

Any wooden object can be painted including secondhand (or new) timber furniture, trunks, closets (easier if the doors can be taken off before painting,) trays and even children's toys. The scope and variety is tremendous, and beginners should not be discouraged from "renovating" some household object as a project.

Metal objects such as trays, old trunks, old watering cans or buckets can also be painted, although the surface preparation is slightly different.

Another common household object popular with folk art painters is the terracotta plant pot; however, it needs to be sealed with clear varnish before basecoating, as the terracotta is very porous and will quickly absorb paint.

WHERE TO PAINT

A place that can be set up on a permanent basis is preferable for serious folk art painters, as it is tedious to have to keep setting up and dismantling equipment every time you wish to paint. A reasonably large table or desk surface is needed, and it should be protected with a plastic cloth or thick sheets of newspaper. Good light is also essential, and adequate ventilation for those times when varnish is being applied.

Opposite: A German-style naïve scene painted dramatically on a vivid red background by Annie Holcombe.

*Russian-style folk
art plate and box
using rich colors
against a black
background.*

STARTING WORK

WITHIN THE TRADITIONS of art are various styles that have evolved according to the culture of the country where they originated. These ethnic styles, in turn, can be interpreted in a purely individual way according to the artist. Although each style has a range of patterns that can be faithfully reproduced, painters need not always stick strictly to an old design, but instead could develop some new designs using the same techniques.

REGIONAL STYLES

Bavarian　　　This style is considered to be the oldest form of folk art. Background colors are generally dark with a contrasting trim, and designs are flat rather than three-dimensional. Bright, primary colors are used.

Dutch　　　Rather formal in design, this style places emphasis on balanced, symmetrical patterns.

Russian　　　Dark, rich backgrounds, bright, primary colors and a highly polished gloss finish comprise this style.

Norwegian　　　There is an emphasis on stroke work with swirls and flowing scrolls.

German　　　Designs are often painted on stained wood, again with bright colors and naive patterns.

North American (Pennsylvanian Dutch) European settlers took with them their folk art traditions characterized by clear colors and a wide range of styles and finishes.

Most important for the beginner is the knowledge that no previous painting experience is necessary to develop the basic skills and techniques quickly. While obviously some people become more adept at mastering brushstrokes and detail, anybody who is interested can rapidly gain confidence and produce works that have a wonderful beauty and individuality.

At first glance, a painted folk art box or plaque may appear quite complex; however, once the elements of design are broken down, they are in fact quite simple and the painting therefore becomes straightforward.

The secret of success when approaching folk art is not to be rigid in either design or technique. Beginners usually stick closely to specific patterns; more experienced painters can become daring and attempt creative ideas. For security, most beginners prefer to trace patterns; however, freehand drawing or painting is often the next step.

To master folk art, follow a few basic rules. Take care of your brushes, keeping them clean and pointed; keep a well organized, clean working area; do not leave lids off paint tubes or cans of varnish; never rush a work, trying to apply a fresh coat of paint before the previous layer has dried; when starting out practice brushstrokes regularly, as the time invested will help you gain control over your hands and fingers.

*The naive qualities
of folk art painting are
demonstrated in this
German Bride's Box,
painted by
Pamela Jones.*

This Norwegian Rogland-style blue plate is a good example of symmetrical patterning.

TECHNIQUES OF THE CRAFT

THE DESIGN and colors which are chosen to decorate an object are purely personal; however, the rich traditions of folk art can be drawn upon to create some distinctive and beautiful patterns and styles. To insure that the creative designs are longlasting and displayed to the best effect, it is important to spend time in preparing the surface to be painted and applying the basecoat before adding the designs, using the different techniques outlined in this chapter.

PREPARATION

Any object to be painted must first be prepared to insure that the surface is smooth and that the paint will adhere.

Secondhand timber objects such as chairs or old trunks will require the most careful surface preparation. A thorough sanding first with medium, then fine textured sandpaper will be needed to remove chipped or peeling paint or varnish surfaces. Some bad surfaces may actually need rubbing back with steel wool to remove previous coats.

After sanding, the surface should be wiped clean and allowed to dry thoroughly before basecoating.

Objects made especially for folk art painting should also be lightly sanded. In some cases where a porous material has been used, such as medium density fiberboard or craftwood, a coat of water-based satin-finish varnish must be applied as a sealer. Otherwise paint will be quickly absorbed into the porous surface, giving a very uneven result. After sealing, lightly sand the edges with steel wool to insure a smooth surface.

Metal objects, both new and secondhand, will also require careful preparation. New metal should first be washed in warm, soapy water, then rinsed with a mixture of equal parts water and vinegar. This cuts back on the oily finish often given to new metal. Before basecoating, the metal should be coated with a special rust-proofing primer. Allow at least 24 hours for the primer to dry before basecoating.

Old metal objects will also need to be sanded back thoroughly with steel wool to remove rust, then coated with a rust-remover. Before basecoating, seal completely with a rust-proofing primer.

BASECOATING

This step is considered vital to the finished look of the work. A sloppy, uneven basecoat will detract from even the best quality painting, so time and care should be invested to create a professional surface.

Use a large brush, applying as many coats as needed to give a smooth, even finish. Quite a lot of paint is needed to give the basecoat depth, so only use enough water to keep the brush moving – too much water will create a wishy-washy effect. Brushstrokes should be smooth, working back and forth in one direction. Always wait until the first coat is completely dry before applying the next – if this is done with care, two coats should be sufficient.

*Timber animal shapes are popular and easy to
paint, like this cow-among-the-daisies.*

Circular boxes and posterboard egg-shapes for painting are available at most hobby stores and specialty art stores.

Never coat only visible surfaces. Back and front, inside and out, should all be given the same even finish!

For a different background effect, consider staining the wood prior to painting, rather than covering the surface with paint. This allows the natural grain to show through, which is wonderful if it is a good quality, grainy wood. Another interesting background treatment is pickling, which gives a faded, whitewashed appearance.

PICKLING

A "pickled" finish can be achieved by mixing equal parts of water-based varnish and a pearlized white acrylic paint and then applying several coats to the project prior to painting the design. There are also commercial pickling preparations available at many hobby stores and home decorating suppliers that give this bleached surface color.

Pickling design

When the basecoat is completely dry, apply the design that is to be painted. The two methods are:

Traced design

For those not confident of their own drawing skills, or those wanting to recapture a particular pattern, designs can be transferred from a folk art pattern book using tracing paper. This paper is semi-transparent and should be placed over the design, which is outlined with a sharp pencil.

The tracing paper is then positioned on the object to be painted, taking care that it is straight and centered exactly in the middle of the surface. Cellophane tape can be used to hold the paper in place while the design is outlined again, leaving a crisp pattern on the timber surface.

If using cellophane tape, peel it away carefully, so as not to damage the basecoat.

Freehand design

Some teachers encourage the use of freehand painting from the first lesson, while others prefer beginners to start with a traced pattern for security.

Freehand painters either first pencil a basic design onto the object to be painted, or start painting directly onto the prepared surface. This technique certainly encourages creative individuality, however, for some newcomers it is a daunting prospect.

When painting freehand it sometimes helps to practice each component of the design, such as a flower or a leaf, on paper first before attempting to paint directly onto the work.

Most freehand painters who do not trace a design onto their work nevertheless work out a design on paper first, to use as a guide.

PAINTING TECHNIQUES

Once the design has been worked out and traced, it is time to start painting. There are several basic brushstrokes that are used repeatedly in folk art, and these should be practiced on paper by the beginner before starting to paint.

Note: With most techniques, the brush must first be dipped in water before being dipped or rolled in the paint. The exception is the "dry shading" technique which requires a dry brush.

COMMA

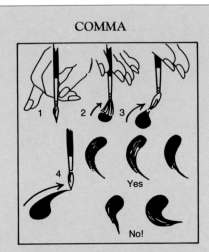

Yes

No!

To paint a traditional comma brushstroke, start by holding the brush upright, at right angles to the work. Gently press down on the bristles so they spread out, making the head of the comma. Gently pull downwards, allowing the bristles to return to a point.

CRESCENT

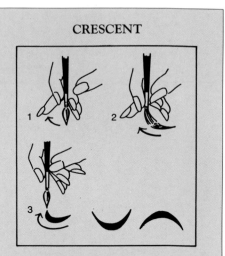

To paint a smooth crescent shape, start on the tip of the brush, which should be at right angles to the work. Use the little finger as a support and gently pull the brush through an arc, gradually adding pressure to splay the bristles. As the brush completes the arc, lighten the pressure, ending again on the point of the brush.

Comma or teardrop stroke

This is achieved by rolling the brush in paint, then holding it upright. Do not lean your hand on the work, but instead try using your little finger to support the brush in an upright position. Push down gently on the bristles, allowing them to form the round head of the comma. Now gently pull the brush downwards in a slight curve, lifting the pressure to allow the brush to return to its natural point. At the end of the stroke, lift the brush off the paper cleanly.

Crescents

Again use your little finger for support, and hold the brush upright. Start with the tip of the brush, then in one, continuous movement, draw a curve applying some pressure to flatten the bristles in the middle of the crescent. Gradually lift the brush, decreasing the pressure and allowing the bristles to regain their natural point.

DOTS

SIDE-LOADING

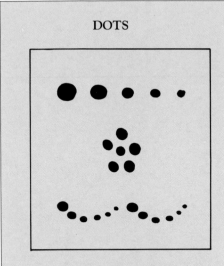

Dots can be made using a wooden skewer, the wooden end of a brush or the head of a pin, depending on the dot size required.

To side-load a brush, first run it through one color, then carefully run one side of the brush through the shading color. Apply the paint in a smooth, even brushstroke to prevent the colors mixing together.

Dots

Some painters use a round brush to make dots, while others use a variety of implements – from a wooden skewer, to a pin head (inserted in a cork) or the wooden end of the brush itself. Some designs call for graduated dots (large to small) and these can be done with a round brush, starting with the largest dot, then gradually getting smaller as the paint on the brush decreases.

Opposite: Traditional folk art painted Christmas decorations, including Advent trees and wreaths.

Side-loading

This technique is much easier than it appears, and produces those wonderful shaded effects that are seen frequently in folk art painting. In reality the brush simply carries two colors or tones at once – generally a lighter and then a darker shade. Use either a round or flat brush, sliding it through one color, then carefully slide one side of the brush into the second, lighter shade. Take care not to mix them together, as the shading effect is created by the two colors side-by-side. Proficient painters can load three colors on the brush at one time, for a really beautiful shading effect.

DRY SHADING

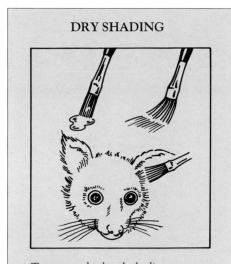

To master dry brush shading, use an old flat brush lightly dipped in paint, without water. Before starting to shade, remove most of the paint by rubbing it on the palette. Use either a scrubbing or skimming motion when applying the paint to achieve a soft, shaded effect.

Dry shading

This method uses an old flat brush that has *not* first been dipped in water. Dip the brush directly into the paint, then wipe most of the paint away on the palette, leaving very little on the brush. Depending on the desired effect, the brush is then skimmed or scrubbed on the surface.

Wet shading

This technique involves the blending of two colors together while they are still wet. Paint the shape required with the darker color, then blend a lighter shade on top as a highlighter. A third shade can also be added, deepening the effect.

Metal objects, like this old-fashioned milk churn, can be painted to great effect. A German-style finish by Irene Raguse.

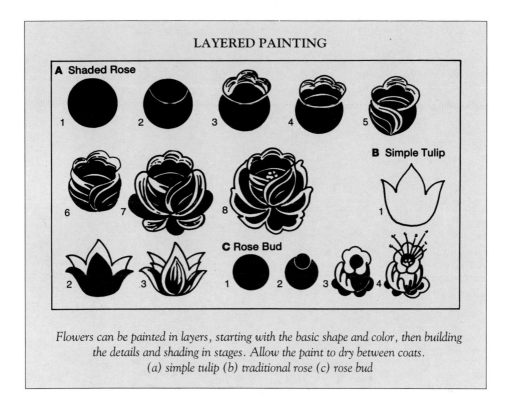

LAYERED PAINTING

A Shaded Rose
1 2 3 4 5
6 7 8

B Simple Tulip
1 2 3

C Rose Bud
1 2 3 4

Flowers can be painted in layers, starting with the basic shape and color, then building the details and shading in stages. Allow the paint to dry between coats.
(a) simple tulip (b) traditional rose (c) rose bud

Layered painting

Beginners may find this method easier than using side-loading or shading techniques. It involves building the painting in various stages. The examples used here show how a simple formula for painting a flower can be easily achieved, starting with a basic shape and then adding colors, shades and tones to create a more complex effect. The same basic method can be applied to any shape – leaves, small animals or birds, even figurative work. With experience, the artist can visualize how the finished painting will look and work out the various stages required to produce that finished effect.

Straight lines

This is the hardest painting technique to master, and requires some practice. Lines are often used for outlining, creating frames or for details such as faces. Use a liner brush and dilute the paint with plenty of water until it is the consistency of ink. Roll the brush in the paint to form a point, then, keeping the brush at right angles to the work, attempt a smooth line. Do not allow paint to accumulate on the brush, or it will form a blob, and do not press too hard – keep to the fine tip of the brush. Practice often to gain confidence.

S-strokes

These are often used for leaves or borders. Use a round brush and begin at the top with light pressure, gradually increasing it as you move into the curve of the "S." As the brush comes out of the curve gradually decrease the pressure until the end.

Borders

Most borders are a combination of linework, dots, commas or S-strokes. Some ideas of the various groupings that can look most effective are illustrated below.

Washes

These involve using a lot of water to thin the paint, giving a translucent effect. A large brush is used for washes if there is a big area to cover.

BORDERS

There are many border patterns based on the comma, teardrop or crescent shape. Fine linework can also be used for a range of borders.

This stylized herdsman in black and red against a timber background is painted in the less commonly seen Hungarian style of folk art.

SPONGING

Use a synthetic sponge dampened with water and then wrung out well. Run the sponge through the paint, then wipe most of the paint away on the palette so there is very little left on the sponge. Practice first on paper to achieve the desired background effect.

SPATTERING

Use an old toothbrush dipped in paint that has been mixed with plenty of water. Wipe away most of the paint with a rag. Use your fingers along the bristles of the brush to spatter the paint. It is a good idea to practice first on paper.

Sponging

A beautiful soft effect is achieved by using a natural sponge lightly dampened with water. Dip the damp sponge into the paint, then remove most of the paint on the palette. There should be very little paint left on the sponge. It is used in various ways, such as smooth circular movements or dabs, to create the desired effect. Sponging can either be done over the basecoat before painting, or after painting before finishing.

Spattering

This is another interesting effect often used as a background, or to soften a piece that looks new, giving it an "antique" look. In this case, the spattering is done after the painting, but prior to the finishing, sealing coat. Use an old toothbrush that has been dipped in a runny solution of paint and water – taking care that the paint does not drip onto the work. Run your finger along the toothbrush bristles so that the light paint mix splatters onto the work.

Articles to be painted can be either practical like this simple tray,
or ornamental like the floral ducks.

CORRECTING MISTAKES

Even the most experienced painters make a mistake from time to time, and these can be corrected in various ways. If the paint is still wet, remove the mistake with a damp cotton swab (it may require several if the mistake is large!) A sharp wooden skewer can be used to scrape wet paint away if a line is inaccurate, and this will give a clean edge or finish. Some mistakes can simply be painted over once they have dried, or at worst sanded back – remember that a new layer of basecoat will need to be applied before painting can resume.

PAINTING TIPS

Keeping your hand relaxed is essential to maintain control and produce smooth, even brushstrokes. This is where practice really helps, as the more repetitions of simple strokes that are performed, the more relaxed the hand will become. Make a mental note to keep the painting hand relaxed at all times. If you feel it tensing up, finish the stroke, then try to relax it before starting the next one.

Different painters approach their projects in a different order or sequence. Some prefer to paint the foliage first, followed by the flowers, then scrolls and borders. Others begin by painting the flowers first, then building outward with foliage, scrolls and borders. There are no strict rules, except that starting in the center and working outward seems to work well for most.

It helps to choose your colors before starting to paint. Do a test sheet of color combinations, then choose those required and squeeze a small amount onto your palette.

FINISHING TECHNIQUES

WHEN the decorative painting is complete, the work must be sealed with a water-based varnish to protect and strengthen the surface.

Always look for a varnish designed specifically for this kind of work, as it will give the most professional finish without discoloring or causing a cloudy effect on dark backgrounds. The varnish should dry in about 15 minutes, and the brushes can be easily washed out in water.

The number of coats of varnish applied will depend on the use of the object. A wall plaque or decorative item needs only four or five coats to give a rich, strong patina to the work. A doorstop, on the other hand, should be given at least eight coats to help it withstand the wear and tear to which it will be subjected.

Items that are to be exposed to either heat or water, such as placemats, trays or coasters, will need to be finished with a polyurethane water-based varnish, to provide the ultimate water- and heat-proof protection. At least four to six coats will be necessary.

VARNISHING TECHNIQUES

Before finishing a work, allow at least one week for the paintwork to cure. If pressed for time, the paint can be dried in front of a heater or with a hair-drier (low to medium setting,) then allowed to cool completely prior to varnishing.

It is important to apply the varnish in thin, even coats using smooth brushstrokes. Use a large brush of good quality for the best results, and to avoid the irritation of hairs dropping from the brush into the varnish.

Always wash the brush thoroughly between coats. For the most even result, alternate the brush direction of each layer, i.e. one layer applied horizontally, the next layer applied vertically. This prevents a build-up of ridges between brushstrokes.

As with the basecoat, the entire object should be covered, top and bottom, inside and out. The time spent will make a difference to the quality of the finished work.

SPECIAL EFFECTS

Some painters like the bright new look of contemporary folk art, while others prefer to "age" their works, giving them a softer, antique appearance. There are several useful methods of creating this look. The technique of patt-ing a damp sponge over the surface to create a soft texture and that of spattering paint were dealt with in "Techniques of the Craft". These methods can both be used after painting has been completed and before finishing. Other interesting aging effects can be achieved by the techniques of antiquing and crackling.

Note: These techniques must be applied before the final varnishing sealing coat.

Opposite: A variety of interesting background treatments and lacy borders for the experienced folk art painter.

Antiquing

This simple finish softens bright colors and gives a patina of age.

First apply a single coat of clear varnish and allow it to dry completely. Next mix one part of burnt umber acrylic paint with three parts of varnish. For a lighter effect add less paint and more varnish; for a darker effect add more paint. Using a large, soft brush apply one smooth coat.

For an interesting shaded effect use a soft, damp cloth to rub the antique finish while it is still wet (this is why the initial undercoat is so important, otherwise the paint could lift.)

Start in the center and work toward the edges of the work, allowing the varnish to remain in places where you require shading, and rubbing it thin in places where a highlight is required.

Allow the antique coat to dry completely before applying further coats of clear finish as described above.

Crackling

This is a marvelous look that again ages the work, giving it the appearance of old paint that has cracked.

A specially formulated crackling mixture is available at most good hobby or folk art stores. It is transparent and should be applied after the painting has been completed, and before the varnish layers are applied.

Items to be given this finish should have been first painted with several good layers of

CRACKLING

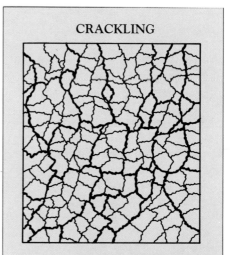

First basecoat the work, applying at least three smooth coats. Insure that the basecoats are dry before applying a generous coat of crackling medium, working quickly and neatly. Avoid touching the surface while the medium is drying. Remember that the crackling effect takes about an hour to become apparent.

An elegant Norwegian box painted with pink and rose flowers against a matte black background.

basecoat to provide a strong foundation. The crackling liquid should be applied thickly and smoothly with a large brush. Work quickly, and avoid going over any areas twice as this will spoil the effect. Do not interfere with this crackling layer while it is drying – it takes about an hour and may appear slow to give the desired finish. But patience will be rewarded. After about an hour the cracks will appear.

Allow this layer to dry completely (overnight) then sand lightly with fine steel wool to remove any ridges or bubbles. Do not use a circular motion, but try and keep this light sanding flowing in the one direction.

Some antiquing mixture can then be rubbed into the cracks for an accentuated effect. Some painters even rub a little gold paint into the cracks, for an extra special effect. When dry, varnish as usual.

BEGINNER'S PROJECT

NAIVE SCENE KEY HOLDER
Designed by Annie Holcombe
of Annie Holcombe's Mountain Living

MATERIALS

Wood piece
Pine key holder available at specialty folk art and hobby stores. Cup hooks to hold keys available at hardware stores.

Palette
Note: *Artist acrylic paints are used in this project. There maybe some variation in the names of the colors depending on the brand.*
Antique white
Naphthol scarlet
Raw sienna
Yellow oxide
Black
Burgundy
Ultramarine blue
Burnt umber
Hookers green
Yellow mid
Silver
Terra cotta

Brushes
Large brush for basecoating and varnishing
No 3 round brush
No 8 flat brush
No 1 round brush
No 1/8 Cormack deerfoot brush

METHOD

STEP ONE
Prepare the surface of the key holder by sanding the wood as necessary.

Apply a basecoat to the top of the key holder only. The side and back can be painted last with a mixture of burgundy and yellow oxide.

STEP TWO
Trace the sky line, paddocks, shed and house. Do not add windows or doors at this stage.

Sky: Mix antique white, a touch of ultramarine blue and a touch of naphthol scarlet. Paint on with a flat brush.

Left paddock: Mix burnt umber and raw sienna.

Right paddock: Mix Hookers green and yellow oxide. You could also add a wash of burnt umber to the green fields. All these may need a couple of coats; wait till the first ones dry before re-coating.

Shed: Use a mixture of black and antique white in three shades: dark, medium and light. Basecoat all the shed in a medium shade and the doorway in a dark shade.

Trace on doorway and windows:

Windows: Medium shade with a touch of burnt umber.

Roof: Silver.

Yards: Medium shade.

NAIVE SCENE KEY HOLDER

Outlines: Dark shade.

Doors: Naphthol scarlet with a touch of burnt umber.

House: Basecoat with a mixture of yellow oxide and antique white. Left side of house a little lighter.

Roof: Silver.

Chimney: Naphthol scarlet.

Smoke: Antique white.

Windows: Yellow oxide, outline burgundy.

Doors: Burgundy, outline with white.

Gutters: Burgundy.

Pathway: Burnt umber.

Fence: White.

Corn and Hayfields: Yellow oxide.

STEP THREE

Trace on trees and animals:

Small trees:

Using a deerfoot brush, paint small trees with a dabbing motion. Use a mixture of different shades of Hookers green, yellow mid and yellow oxide. Do not mix colors together, just pick up a bit of each color and dab.

Trunks: Black.

Large tree:

Trunk: Burnt umber.

Leaves: Use a deerfoot brush again in the same manner as for the small trees. Use a mixture of different shades of terracotta, burgundy and yellow oxide. Dab on terra cotta first, all over the tree. Then burgundy on the

right side of the tree and yellow oxide on the left.

Chickens:
Antique white all over, burnt umber legs and beaks, naphthol scarlet top.

Sheep: Antique white all over. White and yellow oxide mixture and paint small C's over the coat of the sheep, ivory black for the ears, face and feet.

Dog: Burnt umber and white mixture.

Cow: White all over. Black spots, naphthol scarlet and white mixture for the ears and udder.

Straw: Yellow oxide and yellow mid dots.

Fields: A wash of burnt umber over the green fields.

Seed: Yellow oxide and burnt umber.

Bushes: Using the deerfoot brush with hookers green and yellow mid, dab on a variation of green around the house and shed.

Flowers: Dots of all colors.

STEP FOUR

When completely dry, varnish with a satin varnish twice all over. When dry, drill holes for the cup hooks. Then all is finished.

Happy painting!

46

Annie Holcombe's naive country scene is easy to replicate, although colors can be chosen according to taste.

A simple pine plaque is the basis of the beginner's project. It will need to be basecoated and the design transferred onto it prior to painting.

INDEX